A Note from
Mary Pope Osborne About the

MAGIC
TREE HOUSE®
FACT TRACKERS

When I write Magic Tree House® adventures, I love including facts about the times and places Jack and Annie visit. But when readers finish these adventures, I want them to learn even more. So that's why we write a series of nonfiction books that are companions to the fiction titles in the Magic Tree House® series. We call these books Fact Trackers because we love to track the facts! Whether we're researching dinosaurs, pyramids, Pilgrims, sea monsters, or cobras, we're always amazed at how wondrous and surprising the real world is. We want you to experience the same wonder we do—so get out your pencils and notebooks and hit the trail with us. You can be a Magic Tree House® Fact Tracker, too!

Mary Pope Osborne

Here's what kids, parents, and teachers have to say about the Magic Tree House® Fact Trackers:

"They are so good. I can't wait for the next one. All I can say for now is prepare to be amazed!" —Alexander N.

"I have read every Magic Tree House book there is. The [Fact Trackers] are a thrilling way to get more information about the special events in the story." —John R.

"These are fascinating nonfiction books that enhance the magical time-traveling adventures of Jack and Annie. I love these books, especially *American Revolution*. I was learning so much, and I didn't even know it!" —Tori Beth S.

"[They] are an excellent 'behind-the-scenes' look at what the [Magic Tree House fiction] has started in your imagination! You can't buy one without the other; they are such a complement to one another." —Erika N., mom

"Magic Tree House [Fact Trackers] took my children on a journey from Frog Creek, Pennsylvania, to so many significant historical events! The detailed manuals are a remarkable addition to the classic fiction Magic Tree House books we adore!" —Jenny S., mom

"[They] are very useful tools in my classroom, as they allow for students to be part of the planning process. Together, we find facts in the [Fact Trackers] to extend the learning introduced in the fictional companions. Researching and planning classroom activities, such as our class Olympics based on facts found in *Ancient Greece and the Olympics,* help create a genuine love for learning!" —Paula H., teacher

MAGIC TREE HOUSE® FACT TRACKER

Ninjas and Samurai

A NONFICTION COMPANION TO MAGIC TREE HOUSE #5:
Night of the Ninjas

BY MARY POPE OSBORNE
AND NATALIE POPE BOYCE

ILLUSTRATED BY SAL MURDOCCA

A STEPPING STONE BOOK™

Random House ⌂ New York

Random House and the colophon are registered trademarks and A Stepping Stone Book
and the colophon are trademarks of Penguin Random House LLC. Magic Tree House
is a registered trademark of Mary Pope Osborne; used under license.

The Magic Tree House Fact Tracker series was formerly known as
the Magic Tree House Research Guide series.

Visit us on the Web!
SteppingStonesBooks.com
MagicTreeHouse.com
randomhousekids.com

Educators and librarians, for a variety of teaching tools, visit us at
RHTeachersLibrarians.com

Library of Congress Cataloging-in-Publication Data
Osborne, Mary Pope.
Ninjas and samurai : a nonfiction companion to Magic tree house #5 : Night of the ninjas /
by Mary Pope Osborne and Natalie Pope Boyce ; illustrated by Sal Murdocca.
p. cm. — (Magic tree house fact tracker)
ISBN 978-0-385-38632-6 (trade) — ISBN 978-0-385-38633-3 (lib. bdg.) —
ISBN 978-0-385-38634-0 (ebook)
1. Samurai—Japan—History—Juvenile literature. 2. Ninja—Japan—History—Juvenile
literature. I. Boyce, Natalie Pope. II. Murdocca, Sal, illustrator.
III. Osborne, Mary Pope. Night of the Ninjas. IV. Title.
DS827.S3O83 2014 952—dc23 2013043650

Printed in the United States of America
12 11

This book has been officially leveled by using the F&P Text Level Gradient™
Leveling System.

To Joan and Rosie Taylor,
with love

Historical Consultant:

DAVID B. LURIE, associate professor of Japanese history and literature, Department of East Asian Languages and Cultures, Columbia University

Education Consultant:

HEIDI JOHNSON, language acquisition and science education specialist, Bisbee, Arizona

Special thanks to the fine crew at Random House: Heather Palisi; Mallory Loehr; Paula Sadler; Sal Murdocca, a great illustrator; and Diane Landolf, our incredible editor

NINJAS AND SAMURAI

Contents

Dear Readers,

In <u>Night of the Ninjas</u>, we went to ancient Japan and met a ninja master. His wisdom helped us break a spell that had been placed on Morgan le Fay. But first, we had to learn how to act like ninjas. They taught us to follow the ways of nature and how to avoid fierce samurai warriors. It was so exciting to be in the world of the ninjas and samurai that we wanted to learn all about them.

Just like bloodhounds on a trail, we began to track ninja and samurai facts. We found out that samurai warriors played a huge part in Japan's history. They were among the best fighters the world has ever known.

Ninjas were more secretive. They could hide in plain sight and climb up walls in a flash!

After you read about these warriors of ancient Japan, you might not be able to scramble up walls like ninjas or fight like samurai, but you'll have had a lot of fun finding out how they did!

Jack
Annie

1

Ninjas and Samurai in Ancient Japan

If you had lived in Japan hundreds of years ago, you would have seen some amazing sights. Proud samurai warriors with razor-sharp swords glinting in the sun could have galloped by on their horses as you walked down a dusty country road.

And at night, on a narrow village street, maybe you would have spotted a silent ninja climbing up a wall. Who were these

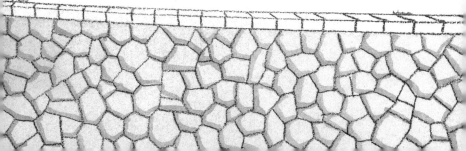

people? And why are they so important in Japanese history?

Ninjas and samurai were some of the most famous fighters the world has ever known. They lived in a time when noble Japanese families, or clans, often fought bloody wars for power and wealth.

Samurai warriors led the clans' armies into battle. Ninjas acted as spies, *assassins*, and explosives experts.

An <u>assassin</u> is someone who kills an important person.

The Causes of War

Japan is a country made up of 6,852 islands, but people live on only 437 of them. The island nation spreads out in a 1,500-mile arc in the Pacific Ocean.

China, Russia, and Korea are Japan's closest neighbors.

Volcanic mountains cover much of the land. Because of the mountains, there aren't many places in Japan where

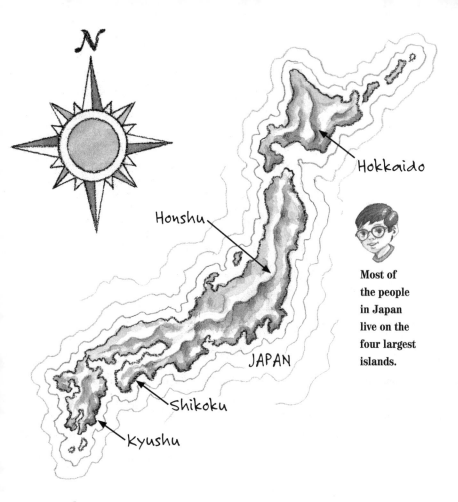

Hokkaido

Honshu

JAPAN

Shikoku

Kyushu

Most of the people in Japan live on the four largest islands.

people can grow crops or live. In the days of the samurai, people usually lived in small fishing or farming villages.

Except for a few rich families, ancient Japanese people were poor. Owning land in a country without much of it meant power and wealth. The more land people owned, the richer and more powerful they became. Wars between different clans over land and power sometimes lasted for many years.

Rule of the Shoguns

The Japanese believed that the emperor came from the sun goddess.

For over twelve centuries, Japan has had an emperor. During the age of the samurai, the emperor wasn't often the true leader of the country. He was a ruler in name only and had little power. In his place, warriors called *shoguns* (SHOW-guns) ruled the land.

Shoguns took power in the late 1100s. By this time, the rule of the emperors had grown weak. As the emperors lost power, the military grew stronger.

In 1192, the emperor gave a samurai, Minamoto Yoritomo, the title of shogun, or general. He asked him to run a separate warrior government. The new shogun set up his headquarters far away from the emperor's court in Kyoto.

Minamoto Yoritomo, the first shogun of Japan

For many of the next 700 years, shoguns were the most powerful leaders in Japan. When a shogun died, his son became the next shogun.

Was his first name Yoritomo?

Yes! In Japan, China, and some other countries, the family name comes first and the person's first name comes last.

Daimyos

While a shogun ran the government, samurai warlords called *daimyos* (DIME-yohz) ruled much of the countryside. Warlords were military leaders with large land holdings. Beginning in the 1300s, there were times when some daimyos had even more power than the shoguns.

The richest daimyos lived in hilltop castles or forts surrounded by villages and

The village around the daimyo's castle was called a <u>castle town</u>.

farms. Down in the villages, merchants and craftsmen worked in their shops. Out in the fields, farmers grew rice, wheat, millet, and barley. For use of the daimyo's land, farmers gave him most of what they grew. Rice was a big part of everyone's diet, and people often paid the daimyo with a *koku* of rice instead of money.

 A koku was the way rice was measured. It was the amount of rice a person would eat in one year. That's about forty gallons!

The practice of landowners letting farmers use their land in return for crops and loyalty is part of what is called the *feudal* (FYOO-dull) system.

Samurai Warriors

The richest daimyos had their own armies. High-ranking samurai served the daimyos by fighting for them. For their work, the daimyos rewarded them with houses, land, and crops. The most-trusted samurai got to live closest to the castle.

Even though there were a lot of wars, at times there were long periods of peace. When the samurai weren't at war, they looked after their estates and enjoyed poetry, painting, drama, gardening, and music.

During the time of knights and castles in Europe, people also lived under a feudal system.

In Japanese, the word <u>samurai</u> originally meant <u>one who serves</u>.

Samurai were like knights in Europe who lived in the age of castles and kings. Like knights, they were devoted to their masters. And like the knights, they vowed to fight and die for them.

Ninjas

By the 1400s, ninjas had become secret fighters for the daimyos. Most ninjas came from farms and villages in the mountains. Daimyos hired them to spy on their enemies. They also used them as weapons and explosives experts.

Ninjas were skilled at getting into places without being seen or heard. They often sneaked out at night while people were sleeping to steal food and weapons or set fires.

Ninjas didn't wear black clothes like

you see in movies or books. In order not to stand out, they dressed like simple farmers or wore disguises.

Even though ninjas wore regular clothes, Japanese art sometimes shows them in dark clothes to give people the idea that they were hard to see. That image remains a popular one today.

 This woodcut print by Katsushika Hokusai dates from 1817.

The age of the samurai and ninjas is a famous chapter in the story of Japan that lasted about 400 years. It was a time when some farmers left their fields to practice *ninjutsu*, the art of secret warfare.

It was a time when samurai warriors were willing to die in hand-to-hand combat for the lords they served.

Turn the page to look inside a samurai castle!

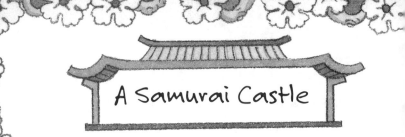

A Samurai Castle

Himeji Castle is a hilltop castle built in 1326 and enlarged in 1600. It's called the White Heron because its white walls and peaked roofs make it look like a watchful bird. Over 3,000 samurai served their lord at this castle.

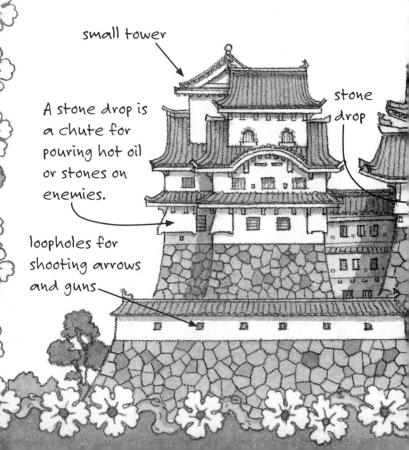

small tower

stone drop

A stone drop is a chute for pouring hot oil or stones on enemies.

loopholes for shooting arrows and guns

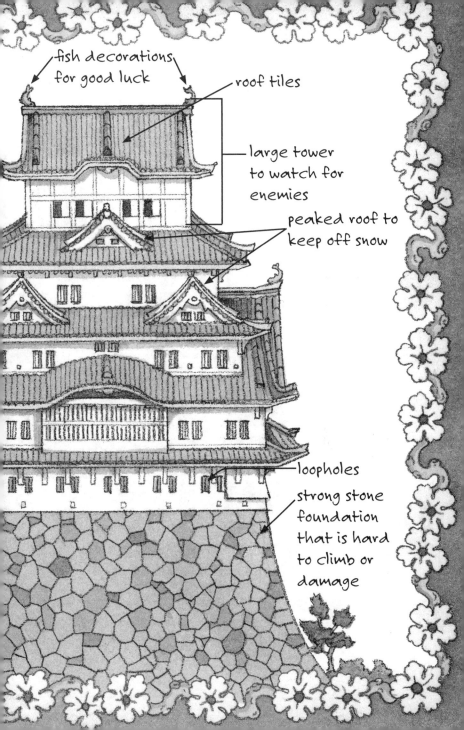

fish decorations for good luck

roof tiles

large tower to watch for enemies

peaked roof to keep off snow

loopholes

strong stone foundation that is hard to climb or damage

2

The Life of a Samurai

To be a samurai, you had to be born into a samurai family. Warfare was a samurai's life, so samurai boys began military training when they were very young. Since the fighting was so brutal, they needed all the skills they could get to survive.

Samurai generals and their armies attacked villages, burned down castles, and killed thousands of people. Much of the fighting was violent hand-to-hand combat.

It was important for a warrior to live and die with honor. The code of the samurai later came to be called *bushido*, or *the way of the warrior*. The word *bushi* means *warrior*.

The Rules of the Samurai

Strict rules guided every moment of a samurai's day. Some were simple. Samurai were expected to get up early, dress neatly, never complain, and have perfect manners. Higher-class warriors also had to learn to read, write, and enjoy the arts.

A samurai's loyalty to his daimyo or shogun was key. He had to put his lord above everyone, including his family and himself.

The code of bushido prepared samurai to die without fear. For them a death in battle was the best death of all.

Rich samurai hired artists to paint beautiful scenes on their walls and doors.

Samurai Families

Everyone in a samurai family followed strict rules. Fathers were the heads of the house.

They taught their children to obey and respect them and all the other adults in the family.

 Japanese students and their teachers greet one another with a bow. Because the teacher is older, she does not bow as low as her students.

Japanese children had to bow when they greeted adults. Today, many still do.

Wives of the samurai played an important part in the samurai way of life. They took care of the family when the men were away and were ready to defend their family if anyone attacked the house. Samurai mothers were proudest of their sons and daughters when they were brave.

Samurai kids learned self-control and manners at a very early age. They weren't allowed to whine or cry. They even had to treat their brothers and sisters with respect!

Before they were five, samurai boys and girls practiced play fighting with wooden swords. Girls learned basic sword fighting, or *kendo*, not for war but to protect their homes.

When boys were around the age of five, their fathers sent them away to study with

Jack Presents: Samurai School

These are some of the things samurai boys had to learn:

Fighting with Swords

When they practiced with real swords, samurai kids didn't get to wear any special clothes or padding for protection. Ouch!

Archery

Boys learned how to shoot a bow and arrow from the back of a galloping horse!

expert teachers to learn the fighting skills
they would need.

Handling a Spear

Samurai boys practiced
fighting with spears of
different shapes and
sizes. It took a lot of
time to learn how to
handle them.

Jujitsu

Samurai boys studied the martial art of
jujitsu (joo-JIT-soo), which is a lot like
wrestling. They learned to pin down
their enemy and keep him
from moving.

A Samurai Home

Hojo Soun was a samurai who lived over 500 years ago. Like other samurai fathers, he had rules for his house. Here are some of them:

1. Go to sleep early and wake up early.
2. Wash in the morning. Don't make a lot of noise, and don't waste water!
3. Show respect to all adults.
4. Practice reading, writing, poetry, and horseback riding.
5. Dress neatly, and fix your hair as soon as you get up. (You never know who's coming to visit.)
6. Tell the truth, and clean up your room!

Reading and Writing

Samurai boys and sometimes girls learned to read and write. This wasn't easy! Japanese writing came from the Chinese script.

The Japanese also have their own letters that are simpler versions of Chinese characters, or symbols.

Each word is almost like a picture.

In order to read Japanese, students must memorize hundreds and hundreds of different characters.

Samurai students spent many hours practicing with brushes dipped in ink. Even when they grew up, samurai practiced the art of writing beautifully. They worked on it all their lives.

Poetry

Samurai children and adults read a lot of poetry, especially short poems called *waka* and *haiku*. Men and women often wrote their own poems and had contests to choose the best.

Here is a haiku by the famous poet Basho, who came from a samurai family.

An old pond:
a frog jumps in—
the sound of water.

Tea Ceremony

Samurai sometimes invited friends for tea ceremonies in their gardens. They sat on straw mats in a simple hut. The

This teahouse is in the old city of Kyoto.

tea ceremony was a time to feel peaceful, away from the cares of the world.

Learning the ceremony took years of study with a tea master. Every movement had a purpose and had to be done very, very slowly.

A tea ceremony could last for four hours!

First the host prepared a special green tea in a bowl. Each guest bowed before taking just three sips. Then they wiped the tea bowl off and passed it on. During the ceremony, there was little talking. Everything and everyone was very calm.

Objects for a tea ceremony include a tea container and a brush to whisk the tea and water together.

Tests of Strength

Samurai teachers tested their students so they would be ready for the harsh life of a warrior.

To force them to be alert at all times, their sword masters surprised them by whacking them with the back of their swords if they looked too relaxed. Samurai were always supposed to be able to defend themselves with very little warning.

A student might have been ordered to walk miles barefoot in the snow or sit for a long time under a freezing waterfall. He also had to go days without eating or sleeping. It wasn't easy being a samurai!

3

Weapons

Samurai were experts at fighting on horse-back and on the ground. To do this well, they needed different kinds of weapons. Early samurai used mainly bows and arrows.

By the eleventh century, the samurai had become experts with swords. In fact, they were probably the greatest swords-men of all time! Several hundred years later, they added cannons and guns.

Bows and Arrows

Warriors shot their arrows with the *yumi*, or longbow. They fired them from the back of galloping horses or on foot. Their bows were made of bamboo or wood.

It took a lot of strength to use a yumi, but the samurai could usually aim and hit their target from about 150 feet away.

Yumi were usually over six feet long!

A samurai had to practice for years before he could shoot well from the back of a galloping horse. He had to drop his horse's reins and grab one arrow after

The rider controlled his horse with his knees.

47

another from his quiver. He brought the bow up to his ear and fired off the arrows with deadly aim.

There were many kinds of arrows. Before a battle, soldiers sent out signal arrows that sounded like whistles. They used them to send messages or to alert the enemy that it was time for the battle to begin. There were also arrows shaped like open scissors to cut through armor. Other arrows sent balls of fire into the air. The most deadly arrows had hooks or barbs on the end of them.

Spears

Spears, or *yari*, were other important weapons. Some were short for close-up fighting. Others were long for fighting at a distance.

Samurai charged the enemy with

their spears. If the enemy attacked, they formed a wall of spears for protection.

Their spears had flat blades that could be between six inches and three feet long. Some spears had such long wooden handles that a samurai on the ground could bring down a soldier on horseback from twenty feet away!

Swords

Samurai used swords along with the bow and arrow. Eventually it became the custom to always carry two swords. The most deadly sword was the longer one, called the *katana*. The smaller was the *wakizashi*.

The two swords together were called daisho, which means big and small.

Samurai were the only people allowed to have these swords. A samurai thought it was an insult when someone touched his sword without asking permission. If he got really mad, he might even kill that person on the spot!

Samurai practiced with their weapons all of their lives.

Soul in the Sword

A sword was not just a weapon to a samurai. It was a magical symbol of all that he stood for. Some even believed that their souls lived in their swords. Losing a sword was a terrible thing.

Samurai even gave their swords special names.

When a samurai boy was born, a small sword was placed in his room. He got his first real sword when he was about thirteen. During his life, he slept with his sword under his pillow. When an old samurai died, his sword was beside his bed.

Sword Makers

While sword makers worked, they wore white robes like Buddhist priests.

Japanese sword makers created the most amazing weapons in history! For them, making a sword was a sacred duty. Before they began work, they fasted and prayed. Making a sword could take many months.

The sword makers' job was to make blades that stayed sharp and wouldn't break. To do this, they hammered layers of soft and hard steel together into thin sheets.

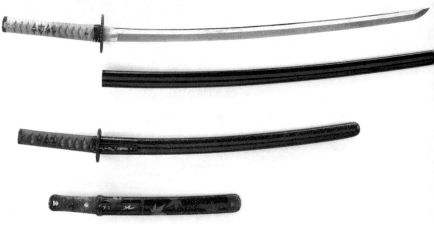

 When they finished, the sword had thousands of very, very thin layers!

The inside was soft enough that it wouldn't snap. The outside was hard enough to remain sharp. Samurai passed their swords down to their sons as family treasures.

Matchlock Guns

In 1543, sailors from Portugal were ship-wrecked on a Japanese island. They showed people their matchlock guns. The Japanese began making these, and soon samurai were fighting with them. Owning a gun was a sign of importance. Warriors often painted their family crests on them. The matchlock was popular for over 300 years.

Matchlock gun

A short time after matchlocks, cannons were added to their lists of weapons. Guns and cannons changed Japanese warfare forever. Instead of fighting face to face, samurai could now fight from a distance.

War Fans

On hot days, samurai cooled off with fans called *gunsen*, which hung from their belts. They had other kinds of fans that they used as weapons or as signals.

At home or when meeting a person of higher rank, a samurai usually didn't carry a sword with him. To be safe, he kept a heavy iron folding fan called a *tessen* at his fingertips.

A tessen was handy for several things. It could act as a shield to ward off arrows or spears. If used as a hand flipper, it made a good swimming aid as well. And if a samurai really needed to, he could throw it at anyone who threatened him. Getting bashed in the head by a heavy iron fan was really painful!

Gumbai were larger fans that didn't fold. They were made of big metal disks. The samurai used them as umbrellas and shields. Commanders also pointed with them to signal their troops.

4

Armor and Battles

Medieval knights in Europe wore very heavy armor. They couldn't run and could hardly walk. Their helmets alone might have weighed over forty pounds!

In many ways, samurai armor worked better than the armor that knights wore. It was light enough to pack up neatly and carry around in a box. It weighed about twenty-five pounds. If need be, a samurai could put on his war gear quickly and race off to fight.

Under the Armor

The first thing samurai put on when dressing for battle was a robe, or *kimono*. Then they pulled on baggy pants and thigh and shin guards. These acted as padding underneath the armor.

The Armor

Samurai armor was made up of small iron scales sewn together with silk cords. A warrior moved easily in it, but it still gave him good protection.

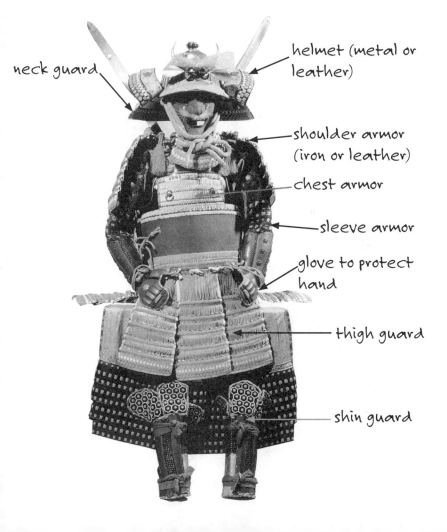

neck guard

helmet (metal or leather)

shoulder armor (iron or leather)

chest armor

sleeve armor

glove to protect hand

thigh guard

shin guard

After taking off his thigh guards, the samurai was able to leap off his horse and climb over walls or wade through rice paddies. If an enemy's weapon cut his armor's silk cords, it could be easily mended.

Headgear

Man-to-man combat in the days of the samurai was brutal. Samurai wore gloves and iron collars for protection from swords, spears, and arrows. They wore an iron face mask as well.

Helmets covered their heads and the back of

their necks. Some helmets were amazing! They were shaped like devils, dragons, rhinoceros horns, and even eggplants!

Hair

To keep their heads cool under their heavy helmets, samurai wore their hair in a top-knot called a *chomage*. Before a battle,

63

The eggplant is a symbol of good luck in Japan.

Sometimes samurai burned incense in their helmets to make them smell good.

they shaved the tops of their heads and left their hair long on the sides.

At times, samurai dyed their teeth black before a battle because they thought white teeth were ugly. They wanted to look their best if they were killed!

Foot Soldiers

When a daimyo decided to go to war, he had to make sure he had enough soldiers. Because of the feudal system, all men and boys under a daimyo's rule were supposed to fight for him if they were able.

The men stopped their work in the fields or shops and signed on for training to be foot soldiers. Foot soldiers didn't ride horses or wear helmets like the samurai. Instead they wore cone-shaped metal hats and fought on the ground, using clubs, spears, bows and arrows, and different kinds of swords.

The samurai got all the glory, but the peasant foot soldiers helped win the wars!

A Battle Begins

Sometimes as many as 30,000 soldiers marched off to battle with their daimyo. The men had little flags sewn on their clothes with their daimyo's colors or symbol. The flags helped the soldiers see who was on their side.

The daimyo and his generals carried large banners so their men could find them. During the fighting, drums and conch shells sounded out calls to the troops telling them what to do.

Samurai preferred to fight in hand-to-hand combat with other samurai of the same rank.

When the samurai arrived on the battle-field, they stepped out one by one to announce how important their families were. Then a samurai from a family just as important as theirs galloped over for a fight.

The daimyo stayed back from the fighting and sent messengers to his commanders. He could see arrows whizzing through the air. He could hear the yells of his men

 Messengers wore flags and huge cloaks called <u>horos</u>, which inflated like balloons when they ran or galloped on horseback.

as they fought. He could also hear the cries of the wounded and dying. At times, the daimyo himself came under attack and needed his bodyguards to protect him.

Turn the page to meet some famous samurai!

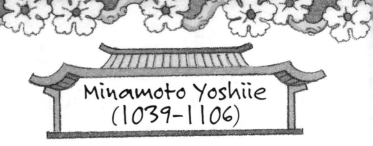

Minamoto Yoshiie
(1039-1106)

Minamoto Yoshiie was a famous samurai who went into battle when he was very young. There is a story that he once chased after an enemy warrior on horseback and dared the man to have a poetry contest with him as they galloped along!

Once Minamoto Yoshiie and his soldiers saw birds circling overhead. First the birds flew down to the ground. Then they quickly flew back up. This made the great warrior suspect that his enemies were hiding in that spot. He quickly ordered his soldiers to surround and attack them. They must have been shocked that he knew their hiding place!

Miyamoto Musashi
(1584–1645)

Some said that Miyamoto Musashi was a very messy samurai who didn't like baths. But he was the greatest swordsman ever! He had a duel with another samurai when he was only thirteen. A duel is when two people agree to fight each other with weapons. Miyamoto Musashi had over sixty duels! He also began a school for sword fighters and tested his skills against other great swordsmen.

For one duel, Miyamoto Musashi quickly made a wooden sword out of a boat oar. After he killed his enemy, he leapt in a boat and rowed away to escape the man's angry friends.

The Yoshioka clan challenged Miyamoto

Musashi to a nighttime duel. He arrived at the meeting place early and hid. When the Yoshioka clan arrived, he jumped out and fought dozens of them with a sword in each hand! Then he cut his way through the rice fields and escaped into the darkness.

Tomoe Gozen
(1157–1247)

There are stories about a brave samurai fighter named Tomoe Gozen. *Gozen* means *lady* in Japanese. Tomoe Gozen was a beautiful woman warrior!

Legend has it that Tomoe Gozen was a great rider, a skilled archer, and a deadly swordswoman.

She is famous for taking part in the Battle of Awazu in 1184. She fought alongside her husband, Minamoto no Yoshinaka, who was battling to control the shogunate. He'd appointed her his head captain. Tomoe Gozen is believed to have been a fierce warrior who cut off the head of at least one enemy.

Minamoto no Yoshinaka died during the battle. Some stories say that Tomoe later married again. Others claim that she became a Buddhist nun and withdrew from the world.

5

The Shadow Warriors

Around the 1400s, daimyos began to look for ways to defeat their enemies without using armies. They started hiring ninjas for jobs that they wanted to be kept secret. Unlike samurai, ninjas didn't devote themselves to just one master. They worked for whoever paid them.

Over the years, there have been folktales about the ninjas' magical powers. Some stories claimed that they were invisible or could turn into animals or fly.

These things aren't true. Over the years it has been hard to learn much about the real ninjas. Because they worked undercover, a big part of their story will probably remain a secret forever.

Who Were the Ninjas?

Ninjas weren't one single fighting group. They came from different clans of mountain people. The mountains cut them off from the rest of the world and kept them from being watched.

The word ninja wasn't used much until about 1964. Traditionally, Japanese called ninjas shinobi, which meant to do secretly.

These tough mountain folk were close to the earth. They grew up knowing the ways of nature. All of this helped them in their work, especially in guerrilla warfare.

Ninjas went to training schools in their villages. There they learned the art of *ninjutsu,* or acting in secrecy. There are stories of ninja girls being trained as well, but no one is sure if this is true.

Ninjutsu

As with the samurai, ninja children came from ninja families. They began to study the art of fighting ninja-style at five or six. At first, the boys played at wrestling and did things like walking across poles to learn balance.

As they got older, their training got stricter. Ninjas didn't need super strength. What they needed was to control their bodies and move without making a sound.

To make their bodies strong and flexible, they did special exercises much like yoga or gymnastics.

Ninja students learned to fight with a wooden staff called a *bo*. They also worked hard at learning how to throw knives, swim, run, and climb ropes.

To practice breaking into buildings, young ninjas climbed high walls and crossed over roofs.

To learn self-control, these ninjas-in-training climbed tall trees and sat in them for a long time without moving.

But that wasn't all! They also learned

how to jump from one high place, such as a building or a tree, to another! And they learned how to make medicines, poison people, and blow someone up with explosives! Yikes!

Ninja students practiced balance and strength by running up narrow boards that were propped against walls.

Smoke and Light

In some movies, ninjas disappear in a puff of smoke. They really had special smoke pots, called *noroshis*. When they lit them, clouds of smoke filled the air, and no one could see what the ninjas were up to. At times, ninjas also set off explosives to distract people.

When ninjas needed light for a job, they carried a bucket with a candle in it. The candle was in a special holder that kept it upright no matter which way they turned the bucket.

If they turned the bucket on its side, the candle gave them enough light so they could set up explosives or draw maps.

If they heard someone coming, they could turn the bucket upside down so the light wouldn't be seen.

Can you spot
the ninja?

6

The Art of
Being Sneaky

Ninjas were experts at fooling people. They often used simple, everyday things for their work.

Sometimes they took a walking stick with them, as many other people did. But because the stick was hollow, they could hide poison darts or knives in it. It took just one quick flick of their wrist to send a deadly weapon on its way!

Ninjas carried medicine boxes that held medicines for themselves and poisons for their enemies.

Kasas

Straw Hats

Japanese farmers often wore a large cone-shaped hat called a *kasa*. These hats were great hiding places for a ninja's knife or arrows. They also hid his face from view.

Flutes

Wandering flute players were also normal sights in feudal Japan. They played long bamboo flutes called *shakuhachis* (shock-ooh-hah-chees). Ninjas usually didn't make

Some Japanese monks who played flutes wore hats like these, and the samurai wore ones made of leather or iron.

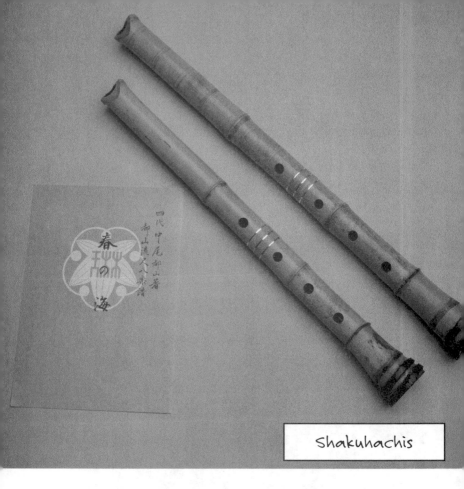

春の海

四代中尾都山著
都山流尺八楽譜

Shakuhachis

music with them. They used them for blow-guns that shot poison darts. Or they banged someone over the head with them!

Chalk and Rice

If a ninja wanted to leave a message for another ninja, he wrote it on a wall with a piece of chalk. After the other ninja read the message, he could easily erase it.

Ninjas could also let other ninjas know where they were going by dropping colored rice on the ground to make trails.

Hiding in Plain Sight

Often a ninja's job was to spy on the enemy and report back to the person who hired him.

When ninjas spied, they had to stay out of sight. Because they were so limber, ninjas could hide in very small spaces. They often curled up into a ball and slowed down their breathing so no one could hear them. They called this quail hiding, because they looked like quails resting on the ground.

Some stories say that ninjas prepared for quail hiding by eating quail eggs!

Trees

Trees also made good hiding places. Ninjas would sit high up in the branches, hidden among the leaves, and stay there for hours. There are some stories that they tied their long sashes between the branches to make hammocks where they could rest without being seen.

Underwater Spying

Hiding underwater isn't easy. When ninjas needed to hide or spy, they sometimes hid in the water.

They gathered up a water plant called duckweed and covered the surface of the water with it. The weeds hid their heads while they were in the water.

Then ninjas could check on their enemies if they happened to pass by. All people saw was a pond covered in weeds. They didn't know a ninja's eyes were watching their every move.

Disguises

Loose priest robes hid their weapons.

Ninjas often wore disguises. Sometimes they looked like Buddhist monks or priests.

Or sometimes they dressed up like women or farmers or flute players. Sometimes they seemed to be merchants with things to sell. If people met a man gathering wood in the forest . . . well, that could be a ninja, too. You just never knew who was a ninja!

The Lantern Trick

In 1558, a group of forty-eight ninjas got into Sawayama Castle by carrying lanterns they'd made to look just like the ones that soldiers in the castle used. Everyone was so confused that it gave the ninjas time to set fire to the castle and escape.

Ninja Business

Ninja families formed guilds, or groups. Each family lived in a certain area and had its own ninja business. Depending on what they did, members of a ninja family had different ranks.

A head ninja, or *jonin*, decided which ninjas should be hired and for what job. He gave orders to his assistants, who planned how the work should be done.

The ninjas who went on the missions were the *genin*. They were the lowest-ranking ninjas and usually came from poor farming families.

At times, the jonin sent his ninjas out to work in teams. They used special codes and passwords to communicate with each other. If the team climbed walls, they made a human ladder with their backs or by standing on each other's shoulders. If one ninja was dangerous, think how scary a team of ninjas could be!

7

Ninja Fighting

Ninjas didn't fight like the samurai. They didn't have a set of rules to follow. They never fought anyone face to face unless there was no choice.

Ninjas struck people from behind by throwing knives or darts from their hiding places. Often their victims didn't know what hit them!

Chigiriki

The *chigiriki* was a hollow stick about two feet long with a chain at the end. The chain had spikes on its tip or a ball with lots of sharp points.

Ninjas used their chigiriki to tangle up their enemy's weapons. They could also hit someone with it and then quickly fit the chain back into the hollow stick. No one knew that a deadly weapon was hidden inside a plain old stick.

Shuriken

Shuriken were sharp pieces of metal that came in different shapes. They made good tools for digging, cutting rope, or removing nails.

Shuriken are also known as throwing stars.

Shuriken could be used as weapons, too. Ninjas could slash someone with their shuriken or throw them to distract people or slow them down. They may have also dipped them in poison and buried them in hopes that an enemy might step on one.

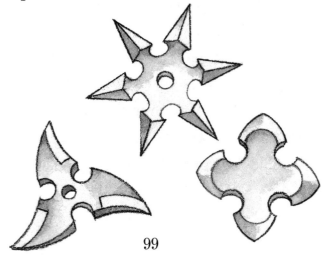

99

Today in Japan there are fukiya clubs where people practice it as a sport.

Fukiya

A *fukiya* was a blowgun about three feet long. Ninjas used them to shoot darts at their victims. Some of the darts were tipped with poison.

It took a lot of practice to use the fukiya. Ninjas worked to be strong enough to hold the gun up for long periods of time. They also learned to control their breath so they could make sure the dart went the right distance. The harder they breathed out, the farther the dart went.

There are stories that ninjas used their blowguns as snorkels when they hid underwater or in the snow.

Ninjas also used the same weapons that regular soldiers used. They were skillful with short swords, knives, bows, battle-axes, and spears. But if they were spotted carrying weapons of any kind, their secret was out!

Nightingale Floors

No one was ever really safe in feudal Japan, even people who lived in the most protected castles. For extra security, they hid weapons all over the place.

To feel safer, people put special floors called nightingale floors in some of their palaces. The floors had nails and hinges that rubbed together when someone walked over them. The rubbing created chirping noises that sounded like birds. The sounds alerted people in the castle when someone was there. Nijo Castle was built nearly 400 years ago. Its nightingale floors are still chirping away today.

8

✴

The End of Ninjas and Samurai

Everything comes to an end. For the ninjas, their end came after a battle over control of their lands. For the samurai, Japan itself changed and became a new nation.

Ninjas began to fade away long before the samurai. They had lived for many years in their mountain villages without control from daimyos or shoguns.

One of the most important ninja clans was the Iga. In 1579, a warlord named Oda

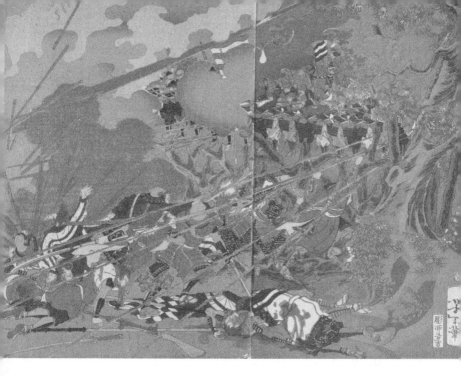

 This print shows another of Oda Nobunaga's great battles.

Nobunaga wanted to rule the Iga ninjas and their lands. But these ninjas heard about his plan. They attacked his castle and burned it down to the ground.

To punish them, in 1581, Oda Nobunaga led 40,000 warriors to fight 4,000 Iga ninjas in their hilltop fort. He and his army attacked from all directions. Though the ninjas fought bravely, the huge army was too much for them.

Oda Nobunaga paid ninjas from another clan to fight with him.

Oda Nobunaga captured the fort and killed many ninjas and their families. The ninjas who escaped made their way to other parts of Japan. This battle ended a time when ninjas were free to rule over themselves. From then on, the ninja way of life gradually disappeared.

End of the Samurai

The samurai lasted longer than the ninjas. But over 400 years ago, Japan began to change. Cities grew, and many people left the countryside to work in them. The samurai began to work in government offices rather than on the battlefield, although their military skills were still important to them.

During this time, the emperor became more powerful than the daimyos.

About 150 years ago, as it became easier to be in touch with other countries, there were many changes in Japan. The shoguns and daimyos lost power. In 1868, the government took away their lands.

With the end of the daimyos, the samurai lost their jobs. In 1876, a new law said that they could no longer carry their precious swords with them. Japan had entered a new world, and it didn't include samurai warriors.

Samurai Today

As the years passed, men from samurai families often became top business and

Many people celebrate samurai heritage at the Autumn Festival in Japan.

government leaders. Today, many Japanese honor their samurai ancestors. They continue to think that honor, hard work, self-control, and respect are the most important things in life.

Some Japanese still perform tea ceremonies and practice many of the old skills like sword fighting and archery. And for fun, Japanese kids watch TV shows and movies about samurai and ninjas.

There are places in Japan today that help people imagine what life was like so long ago. Many samurai castles and teahouses are still standing. They remind us of a time when warriors fought without any fear of death. And they also remind us of a time when ninjas carried out dangerous secret missions in a world that was often at war.

Doing More Research

There's a lot more you can learn about ninjas and samurai. The fun of research is seeing how many different sources you can explore.

Books

Most libraries and bookstores have books about ninjas and samurai.

Here are some things to remember when you're using books for research:

1. You don't have to read the whole book. Check the table of contents and the index to find the topics you're interested in.

2. Write down the name of the book.

When you take notes, make sure you write down the name of the book in your notebook so you can find it again.

3. Never copy exactly from a book.

When you learn something new from a book, put it in your own words.

4. Make sure the book is <u>nonfiction</u>.

Some books tell make-believe stories about ninjas and samurai. Make-believe stories are called *fiction*. They're fun to read, but not good for research.

Research books have facts and tell true stories. They are called *nonfiction*. A librarian or teacher can help you make sure the books you use for research are nonfiction.

Here are some good nonfiction books about ninjas and samurai:

- *Life in Ancient Japan,* Peoples of the Ancient World series, by Hazel Richardson
- *Ninja,* History's Greatest Warriors series, by Sean McDaniel
- *Ninjas: Masters of Stealth and Secrecy,* Way of the Warrior series, by Joanne Mattern
- *Real Ninja* by Stephen Turnbull
- *Real Samurai* by Stephen Turnbull
- *You Wouldn't Want to Be a Samurai!* by Fiona Macdonald

Museums and Japanese Gardens

Many museums and gardens can help you learn more about ancient Japanese culture.

When you go to a museum or garden:

1. Be sure to take your notebook!
Write down anything that catches your interest. Draw pictures, too!

2. Ask questions.
There are almost always people at museums and gardens who can help you find what you're looking for.

3. Check the calendar.
Many museums and Japanese gardens have

special events and activities just for kids!

Here are some museums and gardens that will help you get to know about ninjas, samurai, and ancient Japan:

- Ann and Gabriel Barbier-Mueller Museum (Dallas)

- Asian Art Museum (San Francisco)

- Cranbrook Institute of Science (Bloomfield Hills, Michigan)

- George Walter Vincent Smith Art Museum (Springfield, Massachusetts)

- Metropolitan Museum of Art (New York)

- Museum of Fine Arts (Boston)

- Portland Japanese Garden (Oregon)

DVDs

There are some great nonfiction DVDs about ninjas and samurai. As with books, make sure the DVDs you watch for research are nonfiction!

Check your library or video store for these and other nonfiction titles about ninjas and samurai:

- *Japan: Memoirs of a Secret Empire* from PBS

- *Secrets of the Samurai Sword* from NOVA

The Internet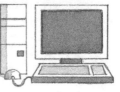

Many websites have lots of facts about ninjas and samurai. Some also have games and activities that can help make learning about ninjas and samurai even more fun.

Ask your teacher or your parents to help you find more websites like these:

- encyclopedia.kids.net.au/page/bu /Bushido

- factmonster.com/encyclopedia /1japhist.html

- samuraikids.com.au/samuraifacts.html

- web-japan.org/kidsweb/explore/history /index.html

Good luck!

Index

Don't miss
Magic Tree House® #5

NIGHT OF THE NINJAS

When the magic tree house whisks
Jack and Annie to ancient Japan, they find
themselves in the cave of a ninja master.
Will they learn the secrets of the ninja?
Or will the samurai warriors get them first?

Magic Tree House®

#1: Dinosaurs Before Dark
#2: The Knight at Dawn
#3: Mummies in the Morning
#4: Pirates Past Noon
#5: Night of the Ninjas
#6: Afternoon on the Amazon
#7: Sunset of the Sabertooth
#8: Midnight on the Moon
#9: Dolphins at Daybreak
#10: Ghost Town at Sundown
#11: Lions at Lunchtime
#12: Polar Bears Past Bedtime
#13: Vacation Under the Volcano
#14: Day of the Dragon King
#15: Viking Ships at Sunrise
#16: Hour of the Olympics
#17: Tonight on the *Titanic*
#18: Buffalo Before Breakfast
#19: Tigers at Twilight
#20: Dingoes at Dinnertime
#21: Civil War on Sunday
#22: Revolutionary War on Wednesday
#23: Twister on Tuesday
#24: Earthquake in the Early Morning
#25: Stage Fright on a Summer Night
#26: Good Morning, Gorillas
#27: Thanksgiving on Thursday
#28: High Tide in Hawaii

Magic Tree House® Merlin Missions

#1: Christmas in Camelot
#2: Haunted Castle on Hallows Eve
#3: Summer of the Sea Serpent
#4: Winter of the Ice Wizard
#5: Carnival at Candlelight
#6: Season of the Sandstorms
#7: Night of the New Magicians
#8: Blizzard of the Blue Moon
#9: Dragon of the Red Dawn
#10: Monday with a Mad Genius
#11: Dark Day in the Deep Sea
#12: Eve of the Emperor Penguin
#13: Moonlight on the Magic Flute
#14: A Good Night for Ghosts
#15: Leprechaun in Late Winter
#16: A Ghost Tale for Christmas Time
#17: A Crazy Day with Cobras
#18: Dogs in the Dead of Night
#19: Abe Lincoln at Last!
#20: A Perfect Time for Pandas
#21: Stallion by Starlight
#22: Hurry Up, Houdini!
#23: High Time for Heroes
#24: Soccer on Sunday
#25: Shadow of the Shark
#26: Balto of the Blue Dawn
#27: Night of the Ninth Dragon

Magic Tree House®
Super Edition

#1: WORLD AT WAR, 1944

Magic Tree House®
Fact Trackers

DINOSAURS
KNIGHTS AND CASTLES
MUMMIES AND PYRAMIDS
PIRATES
RAIN FORESTS
SPACE
TITANIC
TWISTERS AND OTHER TERRIBLE STORMS
DOLPHINS AND SHARKS
ANCIENT GREECE AND THE OLYMPICS
AMERICAN REVOLUTION
SABERTOOTHS AND THE ICE AGE
PILGRIMS
ANCIENT ROME AND POMPEII
TSUNAMIS AND OTHER NATURAL DISASTERS
POLAR BEARS AND THE ARCTIC
SEA MONSTERS
PENGUINS AND ANTARCTICA
LEONARDO DA VINCI
GHOSTS
LEPRECHAUNS AND IRISH FOLKLORE
RAGS AND RICHES: KIDS IN THE TIME OF
    CHARLES DICKENS
SNAKES AND OTHER REPTILES
DOG HEROES
ABRAHAM LINCOLN

PANDAS AND OTHER ENDANGERED SPECIES
HORSE HEROES
HEROES FOR ALL TIMES
SOCCER
NINJAS AND SAMURAI
CHINA: LAND OF THE EMPEROR'S GREAT
    WALL
SHARKS AND OTHER PREDATORS
VIKINGS
DOGSLEDDING AND EXTREME SPORTS
DRAGONS AND MYTHICAL CREATURES
WORLD WAR II

More Magic Tree House®

GAMES AND PUZZLES FROM THE TREE HOUSE
MAGIC TRICKS FROM THE TREE HOUSE
MY MAGIC TREE HOUSE JOURNAL
MAGIC TREE HOUSE SURVIVAL GUIDE
ANIMAL GAMES AND PUZZLES
MAGIC TREE HOUSE INCREDIBLE FACT BOOK